BE GOOD TO YOURSELF

BE GOOD TO YOURSELF.

ESPECIALLY HERE,
AND ESPECIALLY NOW.

LET YOUR NEEDS BE YOUR NEEDS
AND YOUR TRUTH BE YOUR TRUTH.

LET
EVERYTHING
THAT MATTERS
TO YOU

MATTER
TO YOU.

LET YOURSELF
BE ALL THAT YOU ARE.

MAKE ROOM FOR
YOUR COMPLEXITY.

LET YOURSELF BE MORE
THAN YOU USUALLY ALLOW.

YOU HAVE NOTHING TO EXPLAIN TO ANYBODY.

DO NOT SHRINK YOURSELF

TO FIT
ANYTHING
OR ANYONE.

REMEMBER, IT HAS TAKEN YOUR WHOLE ENTIRE LIFE TO BECOME WHO YOU'VE BECOME.

BE FASCINATED WITH EVERYTHING YOU LOVE.

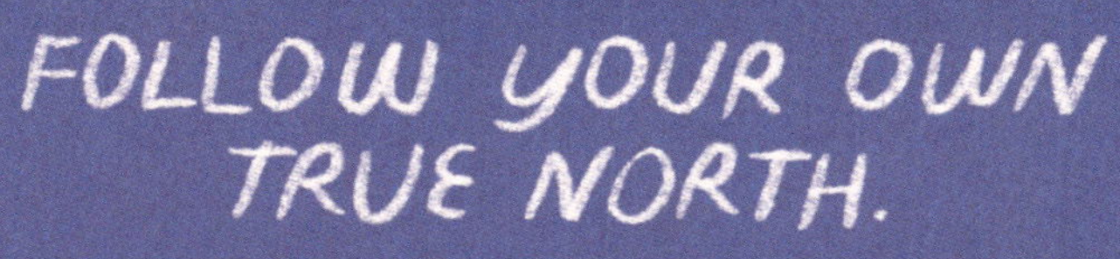
FOLLOW YOUR OWN
TRUE NORTH.

COMMIT
TO
YOURSELF

IN EVERY
WAY
IT COUNTS.

LET YOURSELF
NEED SUPPORT.

LET YOURSELF
BE SHARP,

AND LET YOURSELF
BE SOFT.

LET YOUR JOY
BE VIBRANT
AND FULL
AND COMPLETE.

LET YOUR GRIEF
BE YOUR GRIEF.

AND HOLD IT VERY GENTLY.

BE GOOD TO YOURSELF
WHEN YOU FEEL
YOU'VE LOST YOUR WAY.

HOLD YOURSELF
THROUGH THE
DARKNESS.

AND LOVE YOURSELF
INTO THE LIGHT AGAIN.

LET YOURSELF REMEMBER
THAT IT MATTERS
YOU ARE HERE.

LET YOURSELF
REMEMBER
YOUR PURPOSE.

LET YOURSELF
REMEMBER
YOUR GIFTS.

LET YOURSELF REMEMBER THERE IS MEANING IN THIS WORLD THAT IS READY FOR YOU TO FIND IT.

BE GOOD TO YOURSELF;
YOU ARE WORTHY OF THIS.

HOLD THIS.
KNOW THIS.

BELIEVE THIS.

AND IF THERE'S A PART OF YOU THAT BELIEVES THIS IS NOT TRUE,

BE GOOD TO
THAT PART TOO.

MOST OF ALL,
BE GOOD TO YOURSELF
IN THE TIMES THIS IS
HARDEST TO DO.

BE GOOD TO YOURSELF
BECAUSE PART OF YOU
HAS BEEN WAITING
SO LONG FOR THIS...

TO BE HELD BY YOUR OWN COMPASSION.

TO BE MET WITH YOUR
OWN DEEP TENDERNESS.

SO BE GOOD TO YOURSELF.

ESPECIALLY HERE
AND ESPECIALLY NOW.

REACH DOWN INTO THE HEART
OF YOU AND OFFER YOURSELF
YOUR OWN KINDNESS...

THEN, WITH GRATITUDE,

ALLOW YOURSELF
TO RECEIVE IT.

Written by: M.H. Clark
Illustrated by: Rafaela Pascotto
Edited by: Amelia Riedler
Art Directed by: Jessica Phoenix

Library of Congress Control Number: 2024933851 | ISBN: 978-1-957891-40-8

1st printing. Printed in China with soy and neon inks on FSC®-Mix certified paper.